Occupied

Written by **Sophia Elbouhnini**

Illustrations by **Sophia Elbouhnini and Eleanor Bright**

Fulton Books, Inc.
Meadville, PA

Published by Fulton Books 2021

ISBN 978-1-63710-729-4 (paperback)
ISBN 978-1-63710-730-0 (digital)

Printed in the United States of America

To my amazing mother, for always being there for me when I am sick, need a ride home, or receiving my favorite food. You are loved, kind, smart, and pretty. Thank you for being a great mom! Let's not forget my language arts teacher, Ms. Christy, who influenced me to be creative and to write.

Clouds

Several clouds, low humidity in air,

High air pressure is beneath us,

Cloud condensation nuclei based on puffy different clouds,

No precipitation.

Friends

Frankie

Adventurous, brave

Thinking, grieving, crying

Lonely for her mother's daughter.

Elliot

Kind, funny

Caring, supporting, waiting

Understands ideas with Frankie

Friend.

King (Kilo)

Henry (Hecto)

Died (Deca)

Usally (Unit)

Drinking (Deci)

Chocolate (Centi)

Milk (Milli)

Metric System

Metric, unique, effortless

Measuring, converting, observing

Based on number ten

Systems

Music

Melody, dynamics

Singing, harmonizing, subdividing

Music brings everyone together

Harmony

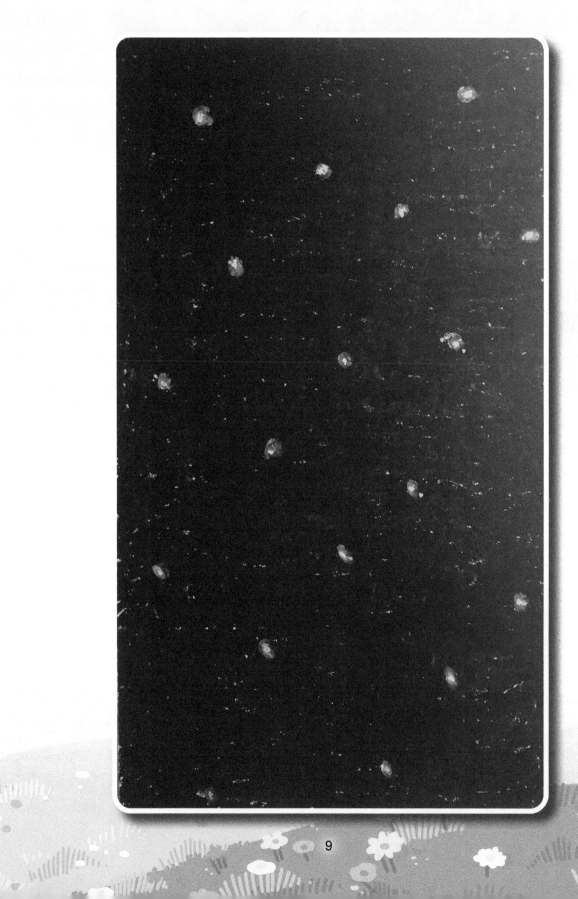

The Night Sky

Outside watching the night sky,

Where the moon shines above the sunrise.

Glowing bright like a diamond on the horizon,

Where the horizon is gleaming toward the golden stars.

Not everyone knows how magnificent the night sky can be,

So that person doesn't have the imagination of three bees.

You know, the night sky isn't just a cloudless, dark skyline.

It's one of the most peaceful things you could ever imagine.

Why does the night sky seem so frightening?

Maybe it's because you only see the treacherous lightning.

The air is fresh and cool, magnificent and colorful, and frigid cold.

Cherish the night sky outside.

Natural Disaster

Tornado

roaring, rumbling

as high as Mount Everest

a dangerous beast moving at a rapid rate

fearful winds blowing objects way up into the exosphere

the terrible thick twisted tornado

yelling at everything that stands in its way

Tornado

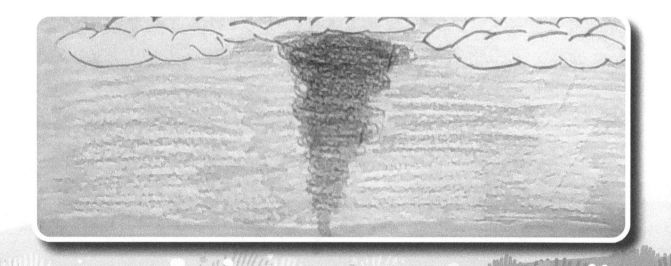

Natural Phenomenon

Birds

chirping, tweeting

graceful like an angel in the bright sky

small soaring planes in the troposphere

so elegant that it could be your wedding dress

beaming, beautiful birds

waving at us from above

Birds

Distance

Boredom takes over my space at home,

Sitting in my cozy, silent warm corner in my room, thinking of what to do next,

People shall find unique ways to be occupied in their beloved homes,

Making scrumptious, creative dishes, in the kitchen next to different objects,

While my little brother's friend says, "What's that strange noise?"

It's me playing the song "Havana" on my violin!

I want to see my friends again,

But all of us have to be patient while we have to observe from afar,

Though it might be a long time, we have to keep what we attain,

As soon as we can have things to do again, as we all used to,

Everything will go back to the way it was.

Trees

In winter,
trees go through
dormancy, which is the
way trees survive in winter. Stale
branches drift onto the frail
ground. Rich brown branches are returning to
a refreshing, warm spring. Spring is here,
new vibrant green leaves begin to return
back to life once again. Temperatures gradually rise,
as it transfers into
summer. The toastiness of the
soil beneath my
feet, the fresh air makes you
believe that summer is coming
soon.
It's summer!
Strong leaves absorb rays of sunlight
and transform the
the energy that lasts decades. Trees
are important, trees contain generations of
ancestry, individuals shouldn't forget.

What My Name Means

My brother thinks my name means "cook me awesome food every day."

My mom thinks my name means "stop worrying on those grades of yours."

My dad thinks my name means "you are not always going to win all your basketball games."

My best friend thinks my name means "you are such an overachiever in everything you do."

My orchestra teacher thinks my name means "make sure to keep your E flats low enough."

My science teacher thinks my name means "try to work hard in our assignment groups."

My neighbor thinks my name means "come over and have some fun."

My dentist thinks my name means "clean teeth every time."

I think my name means "being a genius when it comes to school, and always being happy."

Waves

Small waves on the shore

Salty smells and cold water

Whoosh, whoosh, the waves go

Flowers

Swaying in the sunlight,

Growing and blooming in the spring,

Colors from dark to bright,

And flowers pleasing someone's delight.

Flowers can be used as gifts,

Flowers can be used for moments in time,

Flowers can be used for an assist,

And most of all flowers can be used to reflect someone's life.

Rainbows

When I look up, I see colors,

in the sky. They are red, orange,

yellow, green, blue, indigo, and violet.

Rainbows form when there is sun behind you,

And rain or water in front of you. I say that

rainbows also form when something spectacular occurs in

the world.

Dogs

Soft, fluffy

Running, playing, barking

Giving us daily comfort

Puppies

Family

Family is always there for you,

No matter how terrible the situation you're in.

Family is important in your life,

Which means that they will always be your kin.

Mom

Has been there always

Supports me all the time

I love her so much

Cake

Stirring, baking,

As delicious as cookies

A dessert for special occasions

The fragrance of vanilla coming from the oven

Cake

Summer Leaves

Looking out the window I see summer leaves,

With a pale green color.

I see some leaves that are just brown,

And I see some leaves that are just green.

They slowly fall down to the tough soil,

The season is going into winter soon.

Stars

Bright stars in the

dark, clear sky. They are so

small from one's eye.

When looking up I see the millions of stars floating above.

The stars are lovely and beloved by so many people.

So every time you see the stars at night,

take advantage of these balls of gas in the sky.

Now I want you to go outside

and look at

the stars.

The Beach

Hot sand beneath my feet,
And sitting in my seat.

Smells of the ocean,
With seagulls in motion.

Seashells buried in the sand,
These are all the things that I understand.

Dad

One-of-a-kind dad

Motivating and funny

Brave, clever, and loved

Neighborhood

Fun, inviting

Communicating, enlightening, playing

Having lots of fun

Community

About the Author

Sophia Elbouhnini is thirteen years old, and she attends George Washington Middle School. She has a younger twin brother named Najib. She loves to write poetry because it expresses new and unique feelings. Her hobbies are playing the violin, reading, cooking, and playing sports. When she grows up, she wants to be an orthopedic surgeon and major in chemistry and biology. She wants to be a surgeon because she has a desire to help people and make them feel better. She was exposed to poetry by her sixth-grade English teacher, Ms. Christy. She recognized her talents and encouraged her to continue to write poetry. She wrote this poem book during the COVID-19 pandemic. She asked her friend Eleanor Bright to assist her with the illustrations. Her poetry book will hopefully be a step toward helping people's mental health during the pandemic.

CPSIA information can be obtained
at www.ICGtesting.com
Printed in the USA
BVHW021343070322
630815BV00017B/711